CHOCOLATE CAMELOT

Where the Pain and Sorrow of History
Meet Encouragement and Hope
for the Future

Angela Dawn

Copyright © 2013 Angela Dawn

No part of this document may be reproduced or transmitted in any form or by any means, electronic or mechanical, including photocopying, recording, or by any information storage or retrieval system without the written permission of the author.

Printed in the United States of America

All rights reserved.

ISBN-13: 9781492260974
ISBN-10: 1492260975
Library of Congress Control Number: 2013919752
CreateSpace Independent Publishing Platform
North Charleston, South Carolina

DEDICATION

For my fathers and brothers

Willie Shepherd
Hiram Vaughn
Roy Malone

Alan

Brian	*Maurice*
Dennis	*Michael*
Douglas	*Rodrick*
Duane	*Steven*
Gary	*Wendell*
Kenneth	*Willie*

and all the men, women and children who need to know that someone sees them.

"...I stand before you, but you don't see me. I open my heart, but you don't feel me. You nod your head, but you don't hear me..."
I see you and I understand.

ACKNOWLEDGMENTS

I am extremely grateful to my family and friends for their encouragement and support during this journey, and for lending their insights to the contents in this book. Without your assistance Chocolate Camelot would have been a one-sided perspective.

I especially appreciate Sandra and Latesha for their patience and long-suffering for what seemed to be endless revisions. You helped me keep my sanity.

I would like to extend a very special thank you to Kevin, who served as the impetus for this project. Your timing, as well as your style, is always impeccable.

For those who treat us as equals, "Comrade" is for you.

THANK YOU!

WELCOME TO CHOCOLATE CAMELOT

When a male friend suggested I write something that would uplift Black men, I was honored he thought I would do justice to such a salute. I asked a few men what they would like to hear said about themselves, added what I hoped would be words of encouragement and "Knight in Chocolate Armor" was born. And because we also fight on the battlefield, "Lady Knight" was written. The titles may sound fanciful to some, but I believe they accurately capture the essence of Black men and women in today's society. Since I usually don't have much to say until I begin to write, those poems evolved into Chocolate Camelot.

I have always loved historical romances with castles, knights and ladies, and my favorite medieval tale is of Camelot, King Arthur's castle. A combination fortress and palace, a castle is an extremely secure stronghold and private residence. Lords and princes built castles to control and support the area immediately surrounding them and, as a result, castles served as defense in warfare and symbols of power. Because of the need for such strict vigilance, scouts were assigned to watch for enemy sightings and knights trained constantly and aggressively in preparation to secure boundaries and keep residents safe. Camelot was self-contained, self-reliant and well respected.

Of course King Arthur and Camelot were supposedly created in the imaginations of fiction writers, but that doesn't mean the idea of such a place isn't worth pursuing. Since Camelot essentially symbolizes potential and promise for the future, and Black people have always been a people of potential and promise, the opportunity for Chocolate Camelot is within us.

I am not suggesting that communities take up arms, build walls, or dig a moat—at least, not literally. What I am saying is that we can make our community our castle. If we are individually proactive (instead of reactive) in protecting what is ours by teaching scouts what to look for, training knights how to fight and defend themselves and, most of all, staying vigilant, there is at least the possibility of collectively creating whatever environment we wish.

Unfortunately, there will always be someone who wants to prevent us from having that future. Always! In spite of that reality, history serves to remind us that there was a time when we supported each other, depended upon each other and looked out for each other. In fact, we *were* Camelot. Admittedly our options to do otherwise were limited, but that does not negate the fact that unity is what made our collective success a reality. Only we weren't vigilant…

Today we have the opportunity to choose to be unified, which is by far more powerful in the long term than being bonded by necessity. It begins with believing that Chocolate Camelot is worth fighting for. Camelot must be earned!

Although the poems in this collection are designed for a specific gender or approximate age group as determined by the issues addressed, most of the topics are relevant for anyone of any age in any culture. Please note that wherever "they" is referenced, YOU will know who "they" are based on your knowledge or personal experiences.

It is my desire that these poems will generate conversation and understanding among family members, peers and individuals of all ages, walks of life and cultures. I share my thoughts with you understanding that you may not share my view. That is entirely okay! Writing this tribute to and for us has been a liberating labor of love and I hope that these poems touch your heart as I share mine with you.

Again, welcome to Chocolate Camelot.

CONTENTS

Medieval Titles and Terms

Part One: Master

My Lord Father 3
Knight in Chocolate Armor 7
Nobleman 11
His Lordship 14
M'Lady 16

Part Two: Mistress

My Lady Mother 23
Lady Knight 28
Noblewoman 32
Her Ladyship 35
Armor Bearer 39

Part Three: Knight-in-Training

Squire 45
Battlefield 47
Vision 48
Strategy 50
Arsenal 52

Part Four: Rite of Passage

Page 59
Power Play 61
Accountability 62
Life 64
Champion 66
Currency 67

Part Five: Heir

Little Master 73

Part Six: Lady-in-Waiting

Maid of Honor 79
Solidarity 80
Shield 82
Melanin 83
Depth 85
Precious 87

Part Seven: Coming of Age

Maiden 93
Perception 94
Shade 97
Butterfly 98
Glow 99

Part Eight: Heiress

Little Mistress 105

Part Nine: Honorable Mentions

Torch 111
Knight Inspiration 112
Lady Knight Inspiration 117
Comrade. 121

Citations 127

MEDIEVAL TITLES AND TERMS

Master: Male head of household

My Lord Father: How noble children addressed their father

Knight: Warrior, son of a lord

Nobleman: King, local lord or knight

His Lordship: Term of respect for a nobleman

M'Lady: Form of address for a woman of noble birth

Mistress: Female head of household

My Lady Mother: How noble children addressed their mother

Lady: A noblewoman

Noblewoman: Wife or daughter of a nobleman

Her Ladyship: Form of address for a lady

Armor Bearer: Male attendant bearing the armor of a knight

Squire:	Male, approximately 14-21 years old; generally a noble's son given to a knight to train for knighthood
Page:	Male, approximately 7-14 years old; generally a noble's son given to a knight to be trained
Lady-in-Waiting:	Lady who is attending a queen or princess
Maid of Honor:	Unmarried lady attending a queen or princess; approximately 14-21 years old
Maiden:	Virgin or unmarried girl approximately 7-14 years old

PART ONE

MASTER

MY LORD FATHER

My Lord Father came here on a ship
But it wasn't the Mayflower
Human gold treated as cargo
Dawn of America's darkest hour

You survived the Middle Passage
Death freed many from that indignity
Then watched the hypocritical righteous
Misuse their Bible for indemnity

Branded, chained, whipped at will
Adding insult to indignation
Anything to strip you of humanity
Your welcome to civilization

Naked you stood on the auction block
Gazing beyond the jeering crowd
Myriad thoughts of frustrated rage
Only your eyes could say out loud

Their need to feel superior
Allowed them to treat you as property
Their failure to see themselves in you
Presented quite the dichotomy

They contemptuously called you slothful
As you labored in the field
While sipping on glasses of lemonade
The whip always ready to wield

Fugitive Slave Laws authorized capture
Of runaways willing to brave it
Bounty hunters brought back free men too
All they needed was an affidavit

They acted the way many do
With authority taken but not earned
Their only desire to break you
Cruelty well taught and well learned

It took a civil war to free you
Causing a fury that burns today
Longing for the olden times
When they could force you to obey

Daydreams of darkness and terrors to come
While relaxing on their porches
Thinking how brave hearts beat much faster
Beneath white hoods and torches

From Black Codes to Jim Crow
The beginning of separate but unequal
A new way to strip you of human rights
Making the most of slavery's sequel

The Army War College report
Dismissed you as categorically inferior
Incapable of handling as much pressure
As borne by those deemed your superior[i]

You were classified as immoral
No aspiring to social heights
Best suited to interacting
With only the "lowest class of whites"

CHOCOLATE CAMELOT

White women were your Medusa
You had legitimate reason to fear her
A single glance could kill you
And you didn't have Perseus' mirror

Doctors abused you for forty years
As a guinea pig in their experiment
Allowed a curable disease to ravage your body
Without conscience or sentiment

Fighting against desegregation
They deployed the National Guard
Nine brave children and an armed escort
Wondered why it had to be so hard

Teenagers protesting against Jim Crow
Wanting to make their stand
Police chased with dogs and fire hoses
Showing themselves unmanned

That Sunday didn't start out Bloody
But it sure ended up that way
When you marched for the right to vote
You paid the price you had to pay

Greeted with billy clubs and tear gas
By lawmen newly deputized
The whole world witnessed their brutality
Because this time it was televised

You continued to fight for our lives
While maintaining equanimity
And graciously bore the burden
That was really their ignominy

Your sacrifices taught us survival
Resolution and endurance
Skills we still need to hone today
To face challenges with assurance

The battle continues to be in our minds
We may be weary but not effete
Everything we need is in our DNA
To grasp victory from defeat

Through tears I write this poem to you
For I am your legacy
They tried to kill you with their fear and hate
But you are alive and well in me

My extraordinary Lord Father
Of courage you are the epitome
Take your rest on this hero's pedestal
For the whole of eternity

"Honor your father and mother." (Matthew 19:19a NASB)

KNIGHT IN CHOCOLATE ARMOR

Who are these mighty warriors
These knights in chocolate armor
Bearing the burdens of the world
With such dignity and honor

Always standing at attention
Your character under attack
No one says, "At ease, soldier."
You must be ready to fight back

Challenging the stereotypes
Designed to keep you ostracized
You reach to meet higher standards
Though that rarely gets publicized

Ever in pursuit of knowledge
You know therein lies power
Laying foundation for your renaissance
Abiding in your strong tower

They attempt to steal your identity
And create one of their own
Without understanding who you are
Not knowing you can't be cloned

Often having to prove yourself
For someone to validate you
Even being who they want you to be
Won't transform hearts that hate you

Working hard to earn your pay
An expensive car is a reward
The entitled judge what you should have
By what they can afford

Spend years maintaining your property
Doing things a neighbor should
Still you don't look like you belong
Suspect in your neighborhood

Sometimes you are the sacrifice
That paves the way for others
You do what a man must do
Then extend a hand to your brothers

Every day going into battle
Not knowing what you'll face
Wondering if things will ever change
Always thankful you have God's grace

You can have a Ph.D. in English
Be poignant and eloquent
They will say, "You're so articulate."
As a backhanded compliment

The word itself is not offensive
When stated as a fact
Implicit astonishment is the insult
They think you're oblivious to that

When the playing field is level
Sometimes they feel intimidated
Dare to speak with any authority
They will want you eliminated

Many ancestors fought and died
For the hope of integration
Are you now on the verge of losing yourselves
By sacrificial assimilation?

You try to appear nonthreatening
In your bearing and demeanor
Your quiet dignity offends even more
Occasionally makes them meaner

You fight by holding your self inside
History has taken its toll
Human predators are even more dangerous
When they're no longer in control

Weary backs and wounded souls
Under ashes of notoriety
Rise to take what you have earned
Pride of place in this society

Your lineage is honorable
Garner strength from your past
Fix your gaze beyond the present
To a future you forecast

Unacknowledged soldier
The uniinformed, they scoff
At God's design for armor
That was never meant to come off

Wisdom always as your helmet
Faith and truth your shield
Righteousness your sharpened sword
All ready for you to wield

Hold your head up high and proud
Jaw squared against the sun
March forward on your own terms
You are inferior to no one

I'm proud of you mighty warriors
You knights in chocolate armor
For bearing the burdens of the world
With such dignity and honor

"Be on the alert, stand firm in the faith, act like men, be strong." (I Corinthians 16:13 NASB)

NOBLEMAN

On any given day of the week
When you listen to the news
You hope that day will be different
Maybe hear more balanced views

About men like you who are responsible
Show self-restraint and sobriety
Walk in decency, honor, respectability
Contribute to society
Make your way to work each day
Both college and self-educated
Play does not interfere with business
You go in early and dedicated

Men like you who cherish women
Build up instead of tear down
You take pride in being chivalrous
If they're in sweat pants or a ball gown
Appreciating them as individuals
Knowing each one is not the same
Treating them as if they have value
Not replaceable pawns in a game

Men like you who choose to be faithful
Fully committed to your wives
Daring to stand by philosophies
Others often criticize
Always wearing a knowing smile
Since you could instruct them at length
On how your bond is not one of weakness
Rather one of ultimate strength

Men like you who embrace your role
As leader of your home
Though final decisions lie with you
You know you don't rule alone
Never trying to lead through tyranny
Or even by directive
Love is always the guiding force
Nothing else would be effective

Men like you who educate your sons
About hormones and "come-hither" winks
When squires and maids devalue themselves
It inevitably costs more than they think
You instill within them self-respect
Encourage them to take a stand
Develop character, establish values
Exemplify a righteous man

Men like you who show your daughters
How they should be treated
Ensuring that she knows her worth
Even if called conceited
Emphasizing she pay attention
To what people say and do
Gauging consistency of words and deeds
To determine if hearts are true

Men like you who equip your children
As a result your family respects you
Please know you are highly esteemed
Even if the media neglects you
Battlefield mercy is a rare commodity
Your family is your refuge
Their love for you will heal the hurts
That are caused by subterfuge

Men like you who bend over backwards
So many people you've aided
Without headlines or pats on the back
Or a desire to be feted
Next time you read one of those newspapers
With no mention of men like you
Know that you're not invisible to all
Many of us see what you do

Men like you who are noble men
You are knights in chocolate armor
Who bear your knightly responsibilities
With great dignity and honor

"For the grace of God has appeared, bringing salvation to all men, instructing us to deny ungodliness and worldly desires and to live sensibly, righteously and godly in the present age." (Titus 2:11-12 NASB)

HIS LORDSHIP

I have always admired the way Black men move
Nearly hypnotic, so sexy and smooth
Indulgent as cashmere, sensual as satin
Somewhere there must be a pending patent

On the way you walk, that confident gait
Shoulders squared, unyielding and straight
Each foot planted, you don't play around
Master of your domain, owning that ground

The coolest breeze on a hot summer day
Refreshing my spirit, putting my smile on display
You are impressive my brother. I appreciate your glide.
I wish everyone could see you and feel my pride

Everything about you summed up in your manner
A captivating, mesmerizing personal banner
"I know who I am. Soon you will too.
I'm not here to amuse or pacify you."

Your actions speak for you, you're not a braggart
Inside you is all *The 300* swagger
"Staying in your place" doesn't sit well with you
A man of purpose does what he must do

Resolve in your step, you know where you're going
Determination and fortitude nearly mind blowing
Whether business or personal, you stay on your game
As quiet as it's kept, you only appear to be tame

CHOCOLATE CAMELOT

You haven't been elected, you're not POTUS
Still a side glance tells you everyone's taking notice
You make an entrance without seeking attention
Authenticity has no need for pretension

Magnetism, charm, and a commanding presence
An unanswered challenge to make way for your essence
It woos, persuades, even gives ultimatums
Wherever you are, you bring where you came from

"I will give thanks to You, for I am fearfully and wonderfully made; wonderful are Your works, and my soul knows it very well." (Psalm 139:14 NASB)

M'LADY

When I need to retreat from battle
Drained from the war
My knight is equipped to care for me
Of this I am always sure

You say, "Come to me, M'Lady."
As you gently remove my shield
So that I'm no longer guarded
Free to completely yield

Searching my eyes for clues
To see what I've been through
Taking both my hands in yours
To pull me close to you

You see what no one else can
Because you put yourself aside
Your patience and sincerity
Soothe my wounded pride

You say, "Lean on me, M'Lady."
Though my strength you respect
The fact I'm also fragile
Brings out your desire to protect

Lending me your strength
After being abused and mistreated
Ensuring my diminished reserves
Are never entirely depleted

Your arms offer me sanctuary
A safe place to exhale
Assuring me I'm not alone
That together we prevail

You say, "Talk to me, M'Lady.
My heart is listening.
I'm here to hold you or to help you;
You can tell me anything."

I love the way you love me
My trust you have earned
You bring out the best in me
By using what you've learned

My dreams now have wings
Because you inspire me
You tell me I'm your gift
And how much you admire me

You say, "We are secure, M'Lady.
I am totally committed to us.
Our boundaries are our protection;
No one between or through us.

We belong to each other.
This isn't a question of possession,
But choices and a common goal.
Maybe even a mild obsession."

You offer no apologies
For filling my world with flowers
There's nothing like the scent of love
It strengthens as it overpowers

So when we come from battle
Keeping everyone at bay
You whisper, "Kiss me, M'Lady."
Everything else melts away

"Let his left hand be under my head and his right hand embrace me." (Song of Solomon 2:6 NASB)

Thoughts

PART TWO

MISTRESS

MY LADY MOTHER

My Lady Mother was hauled here
For you, no American Dream
Your agonizing and violent journey
Only the beginning of *The Scream*

Captain and crew took turns raping you
As you crossed The Middle Passage
Your men were chained and forced to watch
Yet they labeled you a savage

Their plan to oppress and disgrace you
Was intended as preparation
To be abused and mauled again and again
By New World civilization

Lady Liberty would not have welcomed you
This was a forced migration
She would not have been a symbol of hope
To escape further subjugation

Standing naked on the auction block
You were sold like a commodity
The self-righteous taunted as they bid
No one saw it as an oddity

Men poked, prodded and molested you
They examined you like cattle
Even young girls were brutalized
You, at any age, were chattel

They successfully repressed their humanity
To prevent themselves from seeing
And ease their mind about atrocities
Committed on a human being

Spit on, berated, tormented publicly
Their humiliating war of attrition
Beating you for the slightest infraction
Yet indignant you'd risk all for sedition

Mostly mulattos worked in the house
Skin color was made significant
A strategy to divide and conquer a people
It was sport to be malevolent

They tried to pervert your sexuality
To avoid accountability for their own
Consumed by frustrated desires
They refused to leave you alone

As they drank whisky and smoked cigars
They ascribed to you promiscuity
To justify their licentious actions
When they raped you with impunity

To nullify the spillage of their seed
They concocted the one drop rule
As if they could biologically whitewash
Their contribution to our gene pool

It took a war between states to free you
Their fury ignites easily today
Longing for those lust filled times
When they could legally force you to lay

When you were enslaved they sold your babies
From your arms they wrenched them
Still forsaking humanity
When that was illegal they lynched them

Some of you managed to pass for white
The first liberated generation
You were able to level the playing field
Exploiting being half their creation

The 1925 War College report
Gave Black "concubines" a pass
To interact with immoral White men
Who otherwise "were considered high class"

They transformed you into Aunt Jemima
As seen through a black face lens
In their stereotyped minstrel shows
With old and new racist pretense

At southern fried chicken and watermelon
They laugh holding on to a mindset
While they inhale fish eggs and clams
With polite society etiquette

From Black Codes to Jim Crow
The beginning of separate but unequal
A new way to strip you of human rights
Making the most of slavery's sequel

No sharing of public facilities
But they gave you their children to raise
While their women sat atop pedestals
Being showered with meaningless praise

You took a stand on a Greyhound bus
Back in nineteen forty-four
Tearing up the sheriff's arrest warrant
And winning in Supreme Court

Sitting politely at Woolworth's counter
Wearing your Sunday best
Enraged patrons assaulted you
Then the police placed you under arrest

They refused to see themselves in you
Wouldn't accept you in their midst
Ambivalent that their ancestors' abuse
Is the reason you exist

Your beauty in strength knows no equal
I am proud to be your legacy
They thought fear and hate would kill you
But you are alive and well in me

Through tears I write this poem to you
The symbol of women's liberation
They set out to destroy your womanhood
Instead you gave birth to a nation

My extraordinary Lady Mother
Your courage has no end
Please rest now upon this pedestal
For you are my heroine

"Honor your father and mother." (Matthew 19:19a NASB)

LADY KNIGHT

Who are these regal lady knights
Secure behind chocolate shields
Guarding against the world's disdain
Striving to ignore how it feels

Ever braced, awaiting battle
Our image under attack
Fighting for and by ourselves
When no one else has our back

No matter the emotion we display
Many will say it is anger
A cowardly strategy of deflection used
By intimates, enemies and strangers

Unacknowledged lady
They would redefine our identity
No grace, no charm, no gentleness
Denying our femininity

Made to feel we're not good enough
We don't receive much validation
Questioning our own self-worth
In search of authentication

CHOCOLATE CAMELOT

When judged by the world's standards
Our beauty is criticized
If we are to believe media reports
Not much about us is prized

Lips too full, ample derriere
Our features unappreciated
Amazing how they become idealized
Once they are imitated

Our hair has texture, tenacity
For this we are mocked and derided
Like its wearer, a force of nature
As much as they try to deny it

Many reminisce about the auction block
As they stare at us, fascinated
Our inherent resilience is legendary
Yet another reason to be hated

They want us to reject ourselves
Forget the truth of what we know
That survival depends on our ability
To distinguish friend from foe

It is possible to confuse the two
When our feelings call on us
So eager to cut someone down to size
That they sometimes fall on us

In the contrived war of light versus dark
Sisters are pitted against each other
Melanin becomes a non-factor
When instead we uplift one another

All of our hues are rich and unique
Each of us specially designed
Neither one superior to the other
Let's get that out of our mind

Velvety smooth and exotic ebony
Supreme empress of mystery
The rarest of jewels in plain sight
One steeped in all our history

Scintillating and intense mahogany
Grand marchioness of purpose
A captivating blend of fire and grace
Hidden depths beneath the surface

Sun-kissed to sun-drenched caramel
Created from an artist's palette
Imperial queen of the Carnaval
Beguiling, impulsive, and passionate

Luminous, radiant, and lustrous ivory
Elegant and chic to behold
Duchess of contrasting, iridescent layers
Shimmering, mischievous and bold

We will never know we are beautiful
If we wait for the world to tell us
Let us blithely ignore negative comparisons
Ultimately designed to quell us

The ability to choose how we feel about us
Is a gift beyond price you know
An obligation of love and privilege
To care for our inner and outer glow

Our beauty is our own to cherish
We don't need anyone's permission
Such diversity is worth celebrating
We need to make that our mission

"Strength and dignity are her clothing, and she smiles at the future." (Proverbs 31:25 NASB)

NOBLEWOMAN

Every morning when you rise
Preparing to face your day
You hope someone will speak admiringly
Instead of another verbal foray

About women like you who are intelligent
Witty, sophisticated and poised
Handle your business efficiently
Without unnecessary drama and noise
Express a depth and range of emotion
Many are perplexed to find
You're willing and able to articulate
The myriad thoughts on your mind

Women like you who honor men
Exalt instead of degrade them
Use your wisdom and understanding
And, when necessary, aid them
Assess each man individually
Don't blame one for another's mistakes
Also hold yourself accountable
Start relationships with a clean slate

Women like you who respect your husband
Take pride in being a wife
The two of you deciding for yourselves
Exactly what you want for your life
You're not ashamed of your femininity
Accept his gallantry with grace
Unabashedly display your love for him
With no concern for saving face

Women like you who work hard to excel
Take pride in whatever you do
Whether a homemaker or an executive
People always depend on you
Working 40 while earning a degree
Still keeping your family together
Sacrificing your present for their future
Leaning on your Rock, your tether

Women like you who educate your sons
About hormones and "come-hither" winks
When squires and maids devalue themselves
It inevitably costs more than they think
You encourage them to be leaders
Assign tasks and responsibilities
Not to make them man of the house
But to nurture their abilities

Women like you who teach your daughters
About "if you loved me you would"
Love does not use, trick or manipulate
You make sure that is understood
Encourage them to think independently
Don't just follow the crowd
People treat you how you let them treat you
They have to define what is allowed

Women like you who invest in your children
You don't let the TV raise them
You nurture, console, guide, instruct
And when doing their best, praise them
You expose them to opportunities
Teach discipline so homework gets done
Make sure they're well-nourished and rested
Set aside time for them to have fun

Women like you who love your community
So many people you've aided
Without headlines or pats on the back
Or a desire to be feted
Next time you see one of those TV shows
With no image of women like you
Know that you're not invisible to all
Many of us see what you do

Women like you who are noblewomen
You hold your chocolate shield high
Ever bending, refusing to break
"But God!" is your battle cry

"The wise woman builds her house, but the foolish tears it down with her own hands." (Proverbs 14:1 NASB)

HER LADYSHIP

I am incredibly awed by the way we love
Often sacrificial, we give everything up
Passionate, compassionate, gentle and intense
Our heart left unguarded, without a defense

Jump in the deep end, put ourselves on the line
Courage and vulnerability delicately intertwine
In spite of the fear we're affectionate and caring
Reach beyond comfort zone, emotionally daring

We invest in our children knowing they're worth it
Confident there's gold, it's our duty to unearth it
Nurture all within reach to ensure they thrive
If we don't mine them they can be buried alive

It's our fierceness and strength that so many rely on
Though we, too, get weak, need a shoulder to cry on
To mask our pain we build a wall high and wide
You need to be strong to risk getting inside

At times we need liberating, a damsel in distress
But oftentimes men come with wounds to address
Guided by providence we can heal each other
By taking the time to truly feel one another

We're sunsets and firelight, elements of nature
Compelling your attention, desiring to cater
A sauna for aches and a potion for fear
Food for your soul, whispers in your ear

Drum beats, rhythms, unrestrained syncopation
Movement and stillness freeing imagination
Massaging your bruises stimulating your mind
While attending to needs of the intimate kind

Cool morning breezes and soft summer rain
The calm in the storm, the ease in your pain
When we walk beside you with our manis and pedis
We are more than decoration, we keep you steady

Hopeful, territorial, loyal to a fault
We may not fight fair when under assault
Dangerous when cornered, of family protective
The intensity of our emotions is never elective

Disrespect is not something we tolerate well
Whether obvious or subtle we immediately rebel
The entitled feel free to do so with impunity
Then shocked our response ignores supposed immunity

We stand up for ourselves and they get indignant
Label us angry Black women to dismiss us as ignorant
Resist any urge to see our humanity clearer
Hypocrisy stares at them through a two-way mirror

Some think color determines where we belong
All it really indicates is we're inordinately strong
It's not black and white and we won't be boxed in
It's about where we are going, not where we've been

Uniquely mysterious, worthy to be explored
A force to be reckoned with, we'll never be ignored
No Y chromosome needed to help refine us
And whatever our shade, hue does not define us

CHOCOLATE CAMELOT

We love to be fashionable, surely no surprise there
Our mood frequently revealed by what we wear
Conservative, alluring or irresistible new trend
They are not us. They don't have to comprehend.

Our hair is our glory and we take that seriously
We care for it like it is a cherished accessory
Each style as distinctive as our own personality
Curly or braided depends on partiality

We are calypso, jazz, rock, rhythm & blues
Romance novel, fantasy or poet's muse
Hustles and hip hop, step, modern and swing
With the right inspiration we can be anything

Cayenne pepper and old school remedies
Honey and lemon and soothing melodies
The cure for our soul is both sour and sweet
And a tantalizing interplay of cool and heat

Defiant, determined, independent of thought
A will of our own that cannot be bought
Go out of our way when someone's in need
Intelligent and capable of taking the lead

We are who we are, but we limit our own power
Identifying with bullies who would have us cower
We owe no apologies for being part of this nation
Rather "you're welcome" for being its foundation

The depth of our faith is continually tested and tried
Scarred knees bear witness to the tears we've cried
But the Comforter brings peace beyond understanding
Even when knocked down, still, we remain standing

It has been a gift to myself to write a poem about us
With so much to offer we can't afford to doubt us
It's through each other we bring our best to the surface
Give meaning to our lives and life to our purpose

"I will give thanks to You, for I am fearfully and wonderfully made; wonderful are Your works, and my soul knows it very well." (Psalm 139:14 NASB)

ARMOR BEARER

When my knight comes in from battle
Exhausted from the war
Your lady is waiting to care for you
Of this you can be sure

Our home will be your refuge
A sanctuary and haven
Who else could provide a healing love
But your adoring steadfast maven

You always deserve my honor
You have also earned my praise
In the battle that you fight for us
You must be determined and brave

Your eyes tell me the stories
That you won't say out loud
My arms are open for you
My breasts will wipe your brow

Bring me your tailor made armor
Especially designed for the wearer
I'm especially designed to care for it
Your tailor made armor bearer

Any polishing or mending needed
Are for invisible marks
Scars buried on the inside
Held closely in the dark

I will gently tend your bruises
Hidden secretly from view
From battles both won and lost
All taking tolls on you

When you falter I encourage you
In success I share your pride
I actively invest in you
I'm not only along for the ride

When you rise I rise with you
A result of natural selection
Shoulder to shoulder, hand in hand
In imperfect perfection

So come to me beloved
My fearsome warrior knight
You and I helped build this land
Side by side we will fight

"The heart of her husband trusts in her, and he will have no lack of gain." (Proverbs 31:11 NASB)

Thoughts

PART THREE

KNIGHT-IN-TRAINING

SQUIRE

The road to chocolate knighthood
Can give you more than blues
Even though you were born to follow it
It's still a path you choose

It may not be the one most traveled
Especially among your peers
Sometimes it seems straight enough
More often than not it veers

Not all squires train with a knight
Some become one on their own
But that doesn't mean no one sees you
And it does not mean you're alone

There are hands reaching out to you
Which you have turned away
Not trusting they could really help
Thinking you'll be okay

Our armor may be strong and durable
It still will be tested and tried
Life is the factory where it's developed
It will scar more than your pride

The truth is we all need guidance
And someone real to talk to
Accepting a hand doesn't make you weak
It lets someone help you walk through

You are loved even if you don't know it
Not necessarily by those who should
Nor perhaps where you are looking for it
But by those who see the good

Your Black is truly beautiful
It is God's gift to this earth
His love for you transcends the physical
It is the passion behind each verse

"I will give thanks to You, for I am fearfully and wonderfully made; wonderful are Your works, and my soul knows it very well." (Psalm 139:14 NASB)

BATTLEFIELD

So where are you headed young squire?
Tell me which war you're fighting
Is it a battle intended to distract you
And has our enemy delighting?

Does it have you killing your brother?
That's not how we're designed
Does it ever make you hate yourself
And play cruel games with your mind?

The enemy uses clever strategies
To prevent you from succeeding
Breaking you down one lie at a time
He is deceptive and misleading

The conflict begins on the inside
Though that's not how it appears
It is designed to pit you against each other
As it plays on all your fears

The fear that no one will ever love you
Care about you or believe
That if you were to die today
Both I and tomorrow would grieve

The mind is the true battlefield
Whoever controls it wins
Give yourself a fighting chance
To determine how your life ends

VISION

Every turning point in life
Will begin with a single decision
Resolve who and what you want to be
Keep that clearly as your vision

Sometimes that can be hard to do
It's so easy to get off track
Especially if you invite drugs into your life
And they won't let you turn back

Many use drugs as a way of escape
When there seems no other way out
They actually trap you in self-destruction
While the enemy watches it play out

Selling drugs may feel like the answer
Easy money, counterfeit respect
But it's you who's being bought and sold
And the future you reject

You are capable of being outstanding
If sound advice you will heed
Respect yourself and your community
Let others follow where you lead

Use your hands for more than texting
Take responsibility for chores
Make a difference in your surroundings
Show you value what is yours

Do the things that make you smile
They help you discover who you are
Be culturally adventurous, even fearless
When adding to your repertoire

Perspective always determines objective
Success won't happen magically
Choose friends wisely, live with purpose
Now you can plan strategically

"It is by his deeds that a lad distinguishes himself if his conduct is pure and right." (Proverbs 20:11 NASB)

STRATEGY

The mere fact of your existence
Makes you extraordinary
With all that is stacked against you
You must be creatively wary

Understanding the why of something
Can be as important as the what
Remember that while on life's journey
You can feel truth in your gut

It begins with comprehending
There are traps laid for you to fail
To discourage you at every step
Because you are young, Black and male

They don't want you to get an education
Or only the very minimal
How else can "solutions" be justified
If they can't call you criminal

If you don't believe knowledge is power
You will always be defenseless
A pawn in someone else's game
Controlled, confined, senseless

Grades may not mean much to you now
But they will when you graduate
They greatly limit or expand your options
And play a huge role in your fate

Even if college is not in your plans
It's not suited for everyone
Explore occupations, develop a skill
You decide what you become

You may have to go in search of people
To give you the guidance you need
You may have to get there on your own
Either way you can succeed

Don't let failure to open one door
Ever stop you from knocking
Your persistence may be the only thing
That keeps a closed door from locking

You have a strength you've yet to discover
One which only comes through trial
Our ancestors proved that conclusively
Using wit, imagination and guile

ARSENAL

I have to decide how I present myself
My style needs to be personal
Trends are fine when I'm with my friends
But I need more than that in my arsenal

When I look in the mirror I should see
Memorable, unique, distinctive
I won't make someone's idea my uniform
What works for me is instinctive

Will pants buckled around my thighs
Get me where I want to go?
Maybe I should pull them up and move forward
Create my own status quo

I know emotions can make me lose control
We all have to learn how to deal
I must change what I put in my mind
To be master of how I feel

Could the reason I get angry so quickly
Be because I invite anger inside?
Regulating who and what influences me
Will keep a lot of drama outside

Record companies make a lot of money
Producing music full of rage
Is it so I can rap my way to my own downfall
One more dead or locked in a cage?

If music can have that much power
I need to use it, not let it abuse me
I'll choose songs that keep me on my path
And watch it affect how someone views me

Thoughts

PART FOUR

RITE OF PASSAGE

PAGE

Chocolate armor is really heavy
Even for a grown man
Now is the time to build your muscles
Pages follow a plan

This chaotic world in which we live
Doesn't seem to have any rules
A lot of people have set them aside
Forgetting they're actually tools

It is very useful for you to know
The language of the street
It is equally important to be adept
At thinking on your feet

Every culture has its slang
This isn't solely about yours
There is a time and place for everything
Learn to use what opens doors

A command of English gives you power
Become friends with a dictionary
A Thesaurus gives you synonyms
To enhance your vocabulary

When you are not interacting
With people from the 'hood
Using words appropriately
Will make sure you're understood

English is the language of business
You need to get that right
Whatever else you want to call it
It is not "talking white"

It is not about being "proper"
It's all about being smart
Your ability to communicate
Gives you an advantageous start

POWER PLAY

Excuse me, please and thank you
Courtesy is simple as that
Good manners impress people
That is an established fact

They show that someone taught you
The true meaning of respect
A little humility goes a long way
You'd be surprised by its effect

Such tools give you options
If you choose them selectively
Sometimes they can control reactions
When you use them effectively

It is not a sign of weakness
Regardless of what "they" say
What it is, is self-control
In other words, a power play

ACCOUNTABILITY

Managing money is extremely important
Whether a dollar or a dime
Save some, spend some, give some back
Like interest, good will is earned over time

It's impossible to ever be too young
To master the ways of finance
Or the ways and means of people with whom
You will someday form an alliance

You'll probably need a loan one day
Here's what you should expect
Bankers only deal in facts
Don't talk to them about prospects

They want to know job, pay, how long
Not interested in cutting you slack
Their primary concern is to make sure
That you can pay the loan back

They'll look into your credit rating
Do you pay your bills on time?
Will you contact them if there's a problem?
Are you financially prime?

You can start work on your rating now
Just do what you say you'll do
Look around to see where you're needed
Do things before they're asked of you

Use your hands for more than texting
Take responsibility for chores
Make a difference in your surroundings
Show you value what is yours

An employer's job is to determine
What you have to offer them
Will you be someone who comes in early
Or someone who always calls in?

Will you represent the company well?
Can you accept it's not about you?
How well do you work with people?
Would they be worse off without you?

If you want to be paid what you're worth
You need to be someone worth paying
Working hard lets you choose your path
It's your future, I'm just saying…

"It is by his deeds that a lad distinguishes himself if his conduct is pure and right." (Proverbs 20:11 NASB)

LIFE

Even though we have been your age
We are not and cannot be you
Sometimes you will need to explain
What you are going through

Talking things over gives perspective
We may both learn something new
We are all designed to need each other
Don't let false pride hinder you

It can be hard to control your emotions
We all have to learn how to deal
You must change what you put in your mind
To be master of how you feel

Why not make music work for you
It can make you feel good inside
When you choose songs to keep you on your path
You will keep a lot of drama outside

Be careful who you let influence you
Everyone is not your friend
If someone tries to give you drugs
That friendship may need to end

CHOCOLATE CAMELOT

The only limits placed on your life
Are those that you allow
Your dreams can become reality
If you take care of the here and now

Learn to use tools wisely
So your armor will be polished and strong
Lessons learned when you are young
Will serve you all life long

CHAMPION

You are designed to be a fighter
Your greatest weapon is your mind
Pick your battles carefully
Leave irrelevant ones behind

Winning and losing are part of life
One coin, opposite sides
Learn to accept both gracefully
Take each one in your stride

Losing any contest is just a loss
It is not a reason for shame
Yes it hurts but succeeding at life
Makes you champion of all games

Let the winner have his trophy
His reward has been justly earned
A Page continues to work toward his dream
Taking stock of what he's learned

CURRENCY

How do I want people to see me
As an individual or stereotype?
It's my responsibility to carry myself
In a way that's more than hype

Trends are fun, they come and go
But what image do I present?
I need to remember clothes are a tool
To facilitate my ascent

Will pants buckled around my thighs
Get me where I want to go?
Maybe I should pull them up and move forward
Create my own status quo

Whenever meeting someone new
I should always hold my head high
Stand straight and shake hands firmly
As I look them in the eye

I go to school so I can learn
My reading, writing and arithmetic
And other academic subjects
To be an example, not a statistic

I can expand my mind in a library
Or in a bookstore take a look
But if I'm not feeling old school
I can always read an e-book

It's smart to be intellectually curious
In life I'll need more than essentials
Then I can make the most of possibilities
That will help me fulfill my potential

Every decision is an opportunity
To be one of a kind or of many
People like to think of me as currency
Will I spend like a bill or a penny?

"I will give thanks to You, for I am fearfully and wonderfully made; wonderful are Your works, and my soul knows it very well." (Psalm 139:14 NASB)

Thoughts

PART FIVE

HEIR

LITTLE MASTER

Little masters make big decisions
Though we have small voices
Even in a single day
My world is filled with choices

I choose to respect myself
To follow certain standards
I won't do what everyone else does
If it means being a bystander

I choose to treat others right
People are more important than things
Even when they seem real tough
Some are fragile as butterfly wings

I choose to forgive people that hurt me
That way I will have peace
Everyone makes mistakes sometimes
I hope they do the same for me

I choose to mean it when I say I'm sorry
Even when I don't want to
I might have to change what I think
So my heart will follow too

I choose to learn everything I can
So I know what I'm talking about
People won't be able to trick me
And fill my head with doubt

I choose to ask lots of questions
That will help others understand
What they think they already know
So we won't all be in quicksand

I choose to lead by example
Especially when others go the wrong way
I will do what I'm supposed to do
Regardless of what they say

I choose to keep playing games
Simply because they're fun
Even when I don't win
It's great to throw, jump or run

I choose to admire an athlete for skill
Respect a man for character
When what he says matches what he does
That will show me he's not an actor

I choose to do what I say I'll do
So that I earn people's trust
They need to know they can count on me
Being steady is a must

I choose to believe I have purpose
That God has a plan for me
That's how I'm going to live my life
To prepare for eternity

Thoughts

"But Jesus said, "Let the children alone, and do not hinder them from coming to Me; for the kingdom of heaven belongs to such as these."" (Matthew 19:14 NASB)

PART SIX

LADY-IN-WAITING

MAID OF HONOR

Caring for your chocolate shield
Requires willpower, self-respect
Faithfully staying true to yourself
Taking time to self-reflect

You will need all of your strength
To become the woman you'd like to be
To resist the urges and temptations
That would keep you from being free

Surround yourself with people
Who when you dream encourage you
Lift you up as you raise them
Rather than discourage you

Society chews up lost young Black girls
They love to call you baby mama
Marketing you as the face of welfare
And the source of all the drama

Don't blindly trust what you hear or see
It's on you to check the statistics
They tell you what they want you to believe
Because they are manipulative and sadistic

Being informed makes you powerful
Now you won't be defenseless
A puppet whose strings will always be pulled
Dominated, confined, senseless

SOLIDARITY

Friends try not to let you do crazy
But regardless of what they say
When your emotions are controlling you
It is easy to be led astray

A video may seem like a good idea
One of you and your sister fighting
An invitation for the world to see
Your pain and frustration igniting

Sometimes we use words like knives
It's our misery overtaking us
Deliberately cutting someone to pieces
Not realizing we're breaking us

The rage that we take out on each other
Keeps the enemy amused
It prevents you from seeing the real battle
Where you have everything to lose

A true friend can be the difference
Between you being a lady-in-waiting
Or becoming a lady of the night
Filled with loathing and self-hating

CHOCOLATE CAMELOT

That might seem like a stretch to you
But it's really a series of choices
Compromising one decision at a time
Ignoring our inner voices

They want us to reject our own
But we thrive by sticking together
History records triumphant tales
Of the many storms we've weathered

SHIELD

Many things will impair your judgment
A brain is as good as your use of it
The greatest gift that has been given to you
Loses power with your abuse of it

Life can become so overwhelming
You look for any means of escape
Someone offers a pill for your pain
Next thing you know you've been raped

Drugs might seem like the solution
Whenever you run out of hope
At first it feels like silk 'round your neck
Until addiction turns it into a rope

Some find themselves on the bargaining table
Trading their body for drugs
No longer controlling their destiny
As the noose gives more urgent tugs

When everyone around you is indulging
They will try to intimidate you
People don't like when you won't do what they do
Even if it eliminates you

The enemy hides in plain sight
But to see him you must pay attention
Sometimes the enemy is a frenemy
Who has their own intentions

MELANIN

You will never know you are beautiful
If you wait for the world to tell you
Feel free to ignore negative comparisons
Ultimately designed to quell you

In the contrived war of light versus dark
Sisters are pitted against each other
To make skin color a source of division
Instead of a bond to one another

All of our hues are rich and unique
Each of us specially designed
Neither one superior to the other
Let's get that out of our mind

Striking and exotic ebony
Intelligence wrapped in mystery
A breathtaking, resilient flowering vine
The beginning of all our history

Warm and intense mahogany
Unexpected as a chocolate bouquet
Irresistibly dramatic and sassy
Whose smile can make your day

Sun-kissed to sun-drenched caramel
An ever blossoming personality
Glowing with charisma and radiance
All merriment and youthful vitality

Luminous and lustrous ivory cream
Stunning and exquisite to behold
A subtle, dramatic centerpiece
Playful, iridescent and bold

Our beauty is our own to cherish
We don't need anyone's permission
It's on us to celebrate our diversity
And change our inner vision

DEPTH

Think about what you'd like to be
If you could be anything you wish
It will take hard work to make it happen
But you gain nothing without risk

Education lets you make better choices
Create unlimited opportunities
You can impact the entire world
Make a difference in any community

You don't have to attend college
There are many ways to learn
You can get a great education
Becoming a volunteer or an intern

Be passionate about something meaningful
It will give you depth and excite
People will want to spend time with you
During the day as well as at night

Learn the art of communication
If you want someone to understand
You can discuss instead of just vent
With your emotions under your command

It's great to have friends and be sociable
But also do things on your own
Helping others gets your mind off yourself
So when older you can handle "alone"

Explore those things that make you smile
They help you discover who you are
Be culturally adventurous, even fearless
When adding to your repertoire

Understanding the why of something
Can be as important as the what
Remember that while on life's journey
You can feel truth in your gut

What you take in is what comes out
Life is not reality TV
Be selective what you allow in your mind
Impress with individuality

You have so much more to offer
Than what you will ever hear
In order to discover it for yourself
You will have to face your fear

The fear that it's true what they say
The world could easily do without you
You exist for the entertainment of others
There's nothing else special about you

That is the furthest thing from the truth
You can change the thoughts in your mind
Build on what God has given you
And you won't need to have it cosigned

"Watch over your heart with all diligence, for from it flow the springs of life." (Proverbs 4:23 NASB)

PRECIOUS

How do I want to present myself
Because advertising really does work
Does my market value go up or down
When my claim to fame is the Twerk?

Sexting someone is more than dangerous
It may seem exciting at the start
But NO ONE is worth risking any action
That might tear my whole world apart

Only users want me to think my body
Has no exceptional value
If I buy the image the media presents
I really won't have a clue

I will thoughtlessly give myself away
Having forgotten that I'm priceless
Seeking attention for attention's sake
And they won't care that I'm in crisis

If I look for love using my body as bait
All I will attract is lust
Love seeks what feeds the heart and mind
And builds intimacy and trust

What should be infamy is now called fame
Regardless of what I've heard
I need to always keep private things private
Embrace modesty as a heart word

When I look in the mirror I need to see
Beloved, cherished and worthy
I won't let someone's idea be my uniform
I'll dress appropriately for my journey

That precious girl staring back at me
Will be grateful for my care
Because sometimes I'll be the only one
Who can see her standing there

"I will give thanks to You, for I am fearfully and wonderfully made; wonderful are Your works, and my soul knows it very well."
(Psalm 139:14 NASB)

Thoughts

PART SEVEN

COMING-OF-AGE

MAIDEN

Your tears break my heart young maiden
They can't be covered by your shield
It's not yet strong enough to hide behind
Or for you to properly wield

I know why your eyes are raining
Someone made you feel unworthy
Not special, not beautiful, not precious
Maybe even a little dirty

Misguided people use any reason
To put other people down
It doesn't matter how good you look
When inside misery abounds

Those who examine themselves
Make a point to lift others up
Those who refuse to face their issues
Abuse you as a cover up

The true shame is not yours to bear
We all have to release our pain
Now dry your eyes and lift your head
You're going to face them once again

But this time you will be armed
With defenses in place and knowledge
You'll be able to keep your head up
Once all that foolishness is abolished

PERCEPTION

I have been where you are, blinded
By what was presented to me
Over the airwaves and in the news
By people who resented me

Part of the reason you feel as you do
Is because it is by design
The decision makers in the media
Have a specific plan in mind

They establish standards of beauty
With magazines and TV
Look around and you will see their truth
Is an invented reality

Flooding every resource with images
That match what they choose to believe
Regulating what you see, read, hear
Thus controlling how all are perceived

Intimidating you into comparing yourself
To ridiculous idealizations
Images they themselves can't live up to
Hold on to that realization

Some look in the mirror and see a flaw
The imagination acts as recorder
Obsessing until an observation becomes
Body Dysmorphic Disorder

CHOCOLATE CAMELOT

From cosmetic surgery to anorexia
They search for physical perfection
See, they don't know their beauty either
Any extreme to avoid rejection

Most of them don't even realize
How they've been exploited too
Believing they are more than they are
Or at the very least greater than you

This manufactured reality
Gives everyone the wrong impression
It caters to those who feel worthwhile
Controlling others by repression

You feel embarrassed by your glory
Because they denigrate it
But we can work wonders with our hair
Causing them to be fascinated

Your color is frequently disparaged
By those with artificially darkened skin
Using your insecurity against you
A tradition of malice carried within

Criticizing the fullness of your lips
Though dissatisfied with their own
Many choose to replicate
That feature when they're grown

Some judge your blended heritage
They won't accept you in their midst
Feeling betrayed that one of their own
Is the reason you exist

All of us are mixed with something
It's merely a question of percentage
Those who mock you should consider that
When they want to dissect your lineage

Standards change from year to year
What once was out is in
You won't fear comparisons
When you develop the person within

Change your thoughts to change emotions
Keep poison out of your heart
Don't let someone's words or actions
Stop you before you start

Perception is a dangerous thing
From a distorted point of view
It can also be a tremendous gift
When it brings clarity to you

"I will give thanks to You, for I am fearfully and wonderfully made; wonderful are Your works, and my soul knows it very well." (Psalm 139:14 NASB)

SHADE

Milk chocolate, ebony, caramel, ivory
Why compare one to the other?
Cocoa is the source for every shade
We all came from the same mother

Know that every person has preferences
It takes nothing away from you
It all makes sense when you realize
That you have preferences too

It's only human nature you know
Liking one thing and not another
It definitely doesn't make one good or bad
Or any better than the other

Always be mindful of your thoughts
Talk back to those inner voices
You are amazing whatever your hue
Remember you have choices

It really all comes down to this
What you decide to believe about you
Fight each negative with a positive
And eventually you won't doubt you

BUTTERFLY

In a garden filled with butterflies
Each one easily holds its own
Together they have a collective splendor
Not one seeks to be a clone

Unique never compares itself
It is proud to be one of a kind
It doesn't pursue those who won't treasure it
Nor does it wait to be defined

Each of our colors are specially created
It is important to celebrate us
They are a bond for our greater good
Not something to separate us

Our beauty is ours to cherish
We don't need anyone's permission
To honor differences that reflect
God's incomparable vision

As with the magnificent butterfly
People will want a closer view
When you embrace who you really are
Accepting the beauty that is you

GLOW

It is my duty to study history
Every culture has its pride
Honor my ancestors' contributions
Not let their legacy be denied

I'll go on a journey in the library
To supplement my education
Omission doesn't mean nonexistent
I have to search for some information

If I learn facts I can reject fiction
The power is all in my mind
I can stop the negative influences
The first step is to press rewind

Knowledge gives me authority to act
To change implied definitions
I am able to set new standards
Decide what deserves recognition

I determine how I present myself
My attire tells a story
They will gladly write my ending for me
If my clothes say I am quarry

I'll create my own description of beauty
It's best to start with the inside
Every philosophy needs a foundation
On which it can abide

Even if everyone told me
I'm more beautiful than any other girl
I'd still have to choose to believe it
To make it a truth in my world

But I'd also be giving them control
Authority over my self-image
Relying on them to build me up
Wondering why I feel so damaged

I get to choose how I feel about me
It's a gift beyond price I know
More than a right, it is a privilege
To care for my inner and outer glow

Being gracious, kind and confident
Shows I'm more than what's on the surface
A special little girl who is on my way
To becoming a young lady of purpose

"Watch over your heart with all diligence, for from it flow the springs of life." (Proverbs 4:23 NASB)

Thoughts

PART EIGHT

HEIRESS

LITTLE MISTRESS

Little mistresses make big decisions
Though we have small voices
Even in a single day
My world is filled with choices

I choose to love my uniqueness
I am specially designed
With my own butterfly beauty
Made to be one of a kind

I choose to protect my body
Everyone is not supposed to see it
It's the only one I've got
It should be the best kept secret

I choose to respect myself
To follow certain standards
I won't do what everyone else does
If it means being a bystander

I choose to be compassionate
A friend to those in need
Especially when others make fun of them
Kindness is more than one good deed

I choose to learn everything I can
Because knowledge is a tool
People will tell you anything
I don't want to be easy to fool

I choose to ask lots of questions
That will help others understand
What they think they already know
So we won't all be in quicksand

I choose to listen to what people say
How they use their words
So I understand their meaning
And not just what I heard

I choose to forgive the mean people
Their pain makes them cruel
I will pray that they get better
And remember the golden rule

I choose to admire an athlete for skill
Respect a woman for character
When what she says matches what she does
That will show me she's not an actor

I choose to tell people what I feel
So they won't have to guess
Then I won't have to get mad at them
For what I didn't express

I choose to believe I have purpose
That God has a plan for me
That's how I'm going to live my life
To prepare for eternity

Thoughts

"But Jesus said, "Let the children alone, and do not hinder them from coming to Me; for the kingdom of heaven belongs to such as these.'" (Matthew 19:14 NASB)

PART NINE

HONORABLE MENTIONS

TORCH

The government may have assigned the month of February as Black History Month, but it is really the responsibility of people who are Black all year long to first know our own history, then teach it to our youth. Reading and learning about people and events relevant to who we are as a culture creates a sense of pride and a desire to not disappoint the living examples of endurance that came before. Our youth need to know that our American journey did not begin with them, but it certainly will only continue through them.

Honorable Mentions is a sample representation of people who managed to be successful despite the barriers placed before them. The information has been put into light verse only to make it more interesting to read. Some of the people mentioned were either born into slavery or not too far removed from it. Where there was nothing, they created it. Where there were barriers, they either broke through or overcame them. Where there were setbacks, they pushed forward anyway. We come not only from survivors, but achievers! Forced migration didn't stop our ancestors and efforts to hold us back won't stop us if we don't allow it!

KNIGHT INSPIRATION

Lemuel Haynes, the first black American
To pastor a white congregation
This Calvinist's writings on universal liberty
Earned him an international reputation[ii]

Reverend William Washington Browne
Had entrepreneurial vision
Founded the True Reformers savings bank
Which included a youth division[iii]

Jan Matzeliger increased shoe production
By inventing the Shoe Lasting Machine
It mechanically attached the "uppers" to soles
Saving millions of dollars for the industry[iv]

Blanche Kelso Bruce was born a slave
Became Republican senator of Mississippi
Fought for the rights of all minority groups
After his term he was Registrar of the Treasury[v]

Daniel Williams opened Provident Hospital
An interracial staff medical facility
It was also a nurses teaching school
Where they were judged only on their ability[vi]

Bass Reeves, from slave to U.S. Marshal
A frontier man, one of the toughest
Once brought 19 men to jail at one time
He's an unsung hero of the West[vii]

All it took was learning the alphabet
And he became an avid reader
Born a slave, died a statesman
Frederick Douglas, abolitionist leader[viii]

Alain Locke, first Black Rhodes Scholar
Writer, educator, and patron of the arts
Philosophical architect of the Harlem Renaissance
The Black perspective he sought to impart[ix]

Jack Johnson fought The "Fight of the Century"
Inspired *My Lord, What a Morning*
The World Champion defeated James J. Jeffries
To put their Great White Hope in mourning[x]

Garrett Augustus Morgan, Sr.
Had only elementary school education
But he rescued workers with a gas mask
He had invented for just such an occasion[xi]

Manager, pitcher, owner Rube Foster
This pioneer gathered his wherewithal
To organize the Negro National League
And become the Father of Black Baseball[xii]

Joyland, the first black owned amusement park
With its Joyland Jazzers and dance halls
Venetian swing, ferris wheel, merry-go-round
An invitation to "come one, come all"[xiii]

David Crosthwait was an inventor
Holds thirty-nine patents for ventilation
He created numerous systems and methods
For heating transfer and refrigeration[xiv]

The Harlem Globetrotters played exhibition games
On Chicago's south side it began
Before NBA integration a star player
Was Wilt "The Stilt" Chamberlain[xv]

Frederick Jones developed box office equipment
That delivered tickets and gave change
He taught himself electronics and was inducted
Into the National Inventors Hall of Fame[xvi]

Jesse Owens, "The Buckeye Bullet"
At the Berlin Olympic Games
Won four gold medals in track and field
History won't forget his name[xvii]

Named for explorer George W. Gibbs
"The first man to set foot in Little America"
Gibbs Point is on the Peninsula
The most northern area of Antarctica[xviii]

He was first Black honored on a postage stamp
This noted educator and author
Booker T. Washington was also first Black
Featured on a Memorial Half Dollar[xix]

Americans called them Redtail Angels
Germans feared the Black Birdmen
They lost few bombers to enemy fighters
Those fearless Tuskegee Airmen[xx]

Charles Houston, scholar and lawyer
Helped found the National Bar Association
Trained Thurgood Marshall and together they
Ended legally sanctioned segregation[xxi]

Ralph Bunche received the Nobel Peace Prize
For mediating Arab, Jew confrontation
Armistice agreements were eventually signed
After eleven months of ceaseless negotiation[xxii]

Jesse B. Blayton, CPA and professor
Acquired WERD radio station
Provided news, music, and community service
To Atlanta's Black population[xxiii]

Henry Lewis transformed New Jersey Symphony
Into a nationally recognized orchestra
This pioneer in the classical music world
Debuted at New York Metropolitan Opera[xxiv]

Arthur Mitchell opened Dance Theatre of Harlem
To provide children in the community
With an introduction to classical ballet
Opening a whole new world of opportunity[xxv]

Arthur Ashe, the first Black male player
In the world to be ranked number one
He is also the first and only Black male
To win U.S. Open and Wimbledon[xxvi]

Ben Carson, the first surgeon to successfully
Separate conjoined Siamese twins
Despite early academic struggles he became
Director of Neurosurgery at Johns Hopkins[xxvii]

Corporate lawyer Reginald F. Lewis
Bought Beatrice International Foods
It became the first black-owned company to have
More than one billion dollars in revenue[xxviii]

Little attention is given to black cowboys
Who made their mark in western history
The Federation of Black Cowboys
Teaches inner city kids their legacy[xxix]

Maurice Ashley founded the Harlem Chess Center
A grandmaster who coaches young players
He is the first Black American to reach that rank
Daily proving wrong naysayers[xxx]

Barack Hussein Obama, our 44th president
In two thousand nine inaugurated
A moment not expected in our lifetime
It was historic and tearfully celebrated

"Let another praise you, and not your own mouth; a stranger, and not your own lips." (Proverbs 27:2 NASB)

LADY KNIGHT INSPIRATION

Madam CJ Walker, daughter of slaves
Built her empire on hair care
She was the first American woman
To become a self-made millionaire[xxxi]

Harriet Tubman, Union scout and spy
Guided the Combahee River Raid
The first woman to lead an armed expedition
Freed 700 South Carolina slaves[xxxii]

Mary McLeod, founder and president
Bethune-Cookman College
Educator and activist, she believed
The key to racial advancement is knowledge[xxxiii]

Sarah E. Goode, furniture store owner
For people living in small apartments
Invented the folding cabinet bed
Complete with supply compartments[xxxiv]

Maggie Lena Walker chartered a bank
At the start of the economic depression
Consolidated all local black-owned banks
Became oldest Black owned operation[xxxv]

The Georgia B. Williams Nursing Home
Owned by midwife Beatrice Borders
The back of the house was a hospital
While the front was her living quarters[xxxvi]

Bessie Coleman learned to fly in France
One of her nicknames was "Queen Bess"
She specialized in stunt flying and parachuting
As America's first Black aviatrix[xxxvii]

Ida B. Wells, Anti-Lynching Crusader
She was an investigative reporter
Editor of the Memphis *Free Speech*
And publisher of *The Red Record*[xxxviii]

Jackie Ormes created *Patty-Jo 'n' Ginger*
A cartoon about a socially-aware child
It inspired the first American Black doll
Whose wardrobe was fashionably styled[xxxix]

She won the Pulitzer Prize for *Annie Allen*
Poet Laureate Gwendolyn Brooks
A little Black girl's view of the world
And her journey into womanhood[xl]

Bessie Blount Griffin, physical therapist
Helped amputees in World War II
Invented an electronic feeding device
Controlled by biting down on the tube[xli]

Annie Easley, NASA rocket scientist
A "computer" before there were machines
Developed software for the Centaur rocket
She was a leading member of the team[xlii]

First Black woman to seek presidency
Shirley Chisholm fought for social justice
Championed minority education
Founding member, Congressional Black Caucus[xliii]

Claretta Simpson with her social security check
Started Career Youth Development Inc.
"Mother Freedom" believed "Love In Action"
Was what was needed in her community[xliv]

Wilma Rudolph "World's Fastest Woman"
National Track and Field Hall of Fame
First female American runner to win
Three gold medals in Olympic Games[xlv]

Grammy Award Winner Elizabeth Cotten
Picked guitar strings upside down
Won "Best Ethnic or Traditional Recording"
With her "cotten picking" sound[xlvi]

Debi Thomas, figure skater, physician
The first Black to medal at Winter Olympics
Wide World of Sports Athlete of the Year
Won national title and World Championship[xlvii]

Dr. Mae Jemison, physician, astronaut
Loves both the sciences and the arts
Founder of two technology companies
Knows that having a dream is just the start[xlviii]

Composer Earnestine Rodgers Robinson
Career began in John 3:16
She became renowned for her oratorios
When instead of reading she began to sing[xlix]

Michelle Obama, Princeton, Harvard graduate
Known as Malia and Sasha's mom
First Black First Lady of the United States
A bastion of impenetrable calm[l]

*"Let another praise you, and not your own mouth;
a stranger, and not your own lips." (Proverbs 27:2 NASB)*

COMRADE

When you say you are color blind, Comrade
I believe I know what you mean
That your heart ultimately enables you
To see us as human beings

That you try not to label individuals
Based on the stereotype
You know character isn't defined
By all the media hype

You don't dismiss us when we tell you
That is not our reality
You concede it's not yours either
And that it breeds enmity

We freely admit that we may not
Care for each other collectively
But that becomes irrelevant
When we assess each other individually

You realize beneath the melanin
And common characteristics
That people are always just people
Unique and individualistic

You don't have to be me to respect
My experience is different from yours
Or to recognize that skin color
Frequently opens or closes doors

You understand that cultural differences
Don't determine one's acumen
They make life much more interesting
Without making one less human

You're able to have a conversation
About the ills of society
Without blaming any one culture
In its absolute entirety

You agree with Thomas Paine's
Rights of Man and Common Sense
That which you demand for yourself
You give others nothing less

You recognize the absurdity
Of one person representing a culture
It's an unfair burden and expectation
Whatever their skin color

You're aware that like role models
Criminals come in all hues
But that the focus is often biased
When you hear the daily news

You don't buy black on black crime
It's called that to foster imagery
Just as with white on white crime
It's all a matter of proximity

You don't tell us to get over it
When we encounter discrimination
Knowing that the torch of racism
Is passed to each generation

CHOCOLATE CAMELOT

All other things being equal
You try to give people a chance
You don't look for reasons to mistreat us
After only a single glance

I want you to know we appreciate you
For treating us with respect
It may not seem like much to you
But it has an exponential effect

We don't mind that you see our exterior
If you see the person within
We can all take pride in our heritage
And be comfortable in our skin

Let's continue working together
Solve unsolved mysteries
Decide to allow new understanding
To create future history

For the whole Law is fulfilled in one word, in the statement, "You shall love your neighbor as yourself." (Galatians 5:14 NASB)

Thoughts

CITATIONS

[i] The Army War College Office of the Commandant (1925), *Employment of Negro Man Power in War*, Franklin D. Roosevelt Presidential Library and Museum, Retrieved Dec 16, 2013 from http://www.fdrlibrary.marist.edu/education/resources/pdfs/tusk_doc_a.pdf

[ii] (2013, March 14), *Lemuel Haynes*, Retrieved Dec 16, 2013 from http://en.wikipedia.org/w/index.php?title=Lemuel_Haynes&oldid=544054434

Taylor, Erica, The Tom Joyner Morning Show (2012, October 28), *Little Known Black History Facts: Lemuel Haynes*, The Black America Web website, (http://blackamericaweb.com/70499/little-known-black-history-fact-lemuel-haynes/)

[iii] Hollie, D. T. Grand Fountain of the United Order of True Reformers. (2012, December 4). In Encyclopedia Virginia. Retrieved from http://www.EncyclopediaVirginia.org/Grand_Fountain_of_the_United_Order_of_True_Reformers.

[iv] Bellis, Mary (n.d.), *Jan Matzeliger (1852-89)*, The About.com Inventors website, (http://inventors.about.com/library/inventors/blmatzeliger.htm)

[v] Taylor, Erica, The Tom Joyner Morning Show (2013, June 17), *Little Known Black History Facts: Blanche Kelso Bruce*, The Black America Web website, (http://blackamericaweb.com/137316/little-known-black-history-fact-blanche-kelso-bruce/2/)

[vi] Daniel Hale Williams. (2013). The Biography Channel website. Retrieved 01:27, Dec 16, 2013, from http://www.biography.com/people/daniel-hale-williams-9532269.

[vii]Taylor, Erica L., The Tom Joyner Morning Show (2013, August 6), *Little Known Black History Facts: Bass Reeves*, The Black America Web website, (http://blackamericaweb.com/154245/little-known-black-history-fact-bass-reeves/)

[viii]Frederick Douglass. (2013). The Biography Channel website. Retrieved 01:37, Dec 16, 2013, from http://www.biography.com/people/frederick-douglass-9278324.

[ix]Alain Locke LeRoy. (2013). The Biography Channel website. Retrieved 01:39, Dec 16, 2013, from http://www.biography.com/people/alain-leroy-locke-37962.

[x]Jack Johnson. (2013). The Biography Channel website. Retrieved 01:42, Dec 16, 2013, from http://www.biography.com/people/jack-johnson-9355980.
Jack Johnson (1878-1946). The About.com Inventors website. Retrieved Dec. 16, 2013, from http://inventors.about.com/library/inventors/blwrench1.htm

[xi]Garrett Morgan. (2013). The Biography Channel website. Retrieved 01:50, Dec 16, 2013, from http://www.biography.com/people/garrett-morgan-9414691.

[xii]*Rube Foster*. (2013). The Biography Channel website. Retrieved 02:14, Dec 16, 2013, from http://www.biography.com/people/rube-foster-9299621.

[xiii]Taylor, Erica, The Tom Joyner Morning Show (May 15, 2013), *Little Known Black History Fact: Joyland Park*, The Black America Web website, (http://blackamericaweb.com/126414/little-known-black-history-fact-joyland-park/)

[xiv]David Nelson Crosthwait Jr. (2013). The Biography Channel website. Retrieved 02:20, Dec 16, 2013, from http://www.biography.com/people/david-nelson-crosthwait-jr-205623.

[xv]Harlem Globetrotters. The Wikipedia website. Retrieved Dec 16, 2013 from http://en.wikipedia.org/wiki/Harlem_Globetrotters

[xvi]Bellis, Mary, *Frederick Jones (1893-1961)*, The About.com Inventors website, Retrieved Dec 16, 2013 from http://inventors.about.com/library/inventors/blf_jones.htm

[xvii]Taylor, Erica L., The Tom Joyner Morning Show (2013, October 13), *Little Known Black History Fact: The Jesse Owens High School*, The Black America Web website, (http://blackamericaweb.com/173467/little-known-black-history-fact-the-jesse-owens-high-school/)

Jesse Owens. (2013). The Biography Channel website. Retrieved 02:33, Dec 16, 2013, from http://www.biography.com/people/jesse-owens-9431142.

[xviii]*George W. Gibbs, Jr.* The Wikipedia website. Retrieved Dec 16, 2013 from http://en.wikipedia.org/wiki/George_W._Gibbs,_Jr.

[xix]Booker T. Washington. The Wikipedia website. Retrieved Dec 16, 2013 from http://en.wikipedia.org/wiki/Booker_T._Washington

[xx]Rominger, Tyler. LV Veterans History Project (2012). *The Tuskegee Airmen*, Retrieved Dec 16, 2013 from http://www.lvveteranshistory.org/the-tuskegee-airmen/

[xxi]*NAACP History: Charles Hamilton Houston.* Retrieved Dec 16, 2013 from http://www.naacp.org/pages/naacp-history-charles-hamilton-houston

[xxii]"Ralph Bunche - Biographical". Nobelprize.org. Nobel Media AB 2013. Web. 16 Dec 2013. <http://www.nobelprize.org/nobel_prizes/peace/laureates/1950/bunche-bio.html>

[xxiii]Halper, Donna L. (2008), *The First African-American Radio Station Owner: Jesse B. Blayton Sr.*, (http://www.lwfaah.net/aaradio/1staa_radio.htm)

[xxiv]Jones, Joyce (2013), *This Day in Black History: Feb. 15, 1968*, The BET website, (http://www.bet.com/news/national/2013/02/15/this-day-in-black-history-feb-15-1968.html)

[xxv](2012), *Legacy*, The Dance Theatre of Harlem website, Retrieved Dec 16, 2013 from http://www.dancetheatreofharlem.org/legacy

[xxvi]Arthur Ashe. (2013). The Biography Channel website. Retrieved 03:21, Dec 16, 2013, from http://www.biography.com/people/arthur-ashe-9190544.

[xxvii]Ben Carson. (2013). The Biography Channel website. Retrieved 03:28, Dec 16, 2013, from http://www.biography.com/people/ben-carson-475422.

[xxviii]Edmond, Alfred, Off My Chest (2012, November 30), *I'm Proud to Be Part of the Legacy of Reginald F. Lewis*, (http://www.blackenterprise.com/blogs/im-proud-to-be-part-of-the-legacy-of-reginald-f-lewis/)

(2012-2013), Reginald F. Lewis, (http://www.rflewismuseum.org/about/reginald-lewis)

[xxix]Taylor, Erica, The Tom Joyner Morning Show (2012, November 19), *Little Known Black History Facts: Black Cowboys*, The Black America Web website, (http://blackamericaweb.com/73754/little-known-black-history-fact-black-cowboys/2/)

[xxx]The New York Times (1999, December 29) *In Harlem, a Chess Champion Passes On His Moves and Enthusiasm*, Retrieved Dec 16, 2013 from http://www.nytimes.com/1999/12/29/nyregion/in-harlem-a-chess-champion-passes-on-his-moves-and-enthusiasm.html?pagewanted=2&src=pm

[xxxi]Bellis, Mary, *Madame C.J. Walker (1867-1919)*, The About.com Inventors website, Retrieved Dec 16, 2013 from http://inventors.about.com/od/wstartinventors/a/MadameWalker.htm

[xxxii]Patterson, Tiffany R. L., History, *Harriet Tubman*, Retrieved Dec 16, 2013 from http://www.history.com/topics/harriet-tubman

LeSourd, Nancy, *Harriet Tubman: Civil War Spy, Daring Soldier*, The Liberty Letters website, Retrieved Dec 16, 2003 from http://www.libertyletters.com/resources/civil-war/harriet-tubman-civil-war-spy.php

Patterson, Tiffany R. L., History, *Harriet Tubman*, Retrieved Dec 16, 2013 from http://www.history.com/topics/harriet-tubman

[xxxiii]Mary McLeod Bethune. (2013). The Biography Channel website. Retrieved 05:14, Dec 17, 2013, from http://www.biography.com/people/mary-mcleod-bethune-9211266.

[xxxiv]Sarah E. Goode. (2013). The Biography Channel website. Retrieved 04:11, Dec 16, 2013, from http://www.biography.com/people/sarah-e-goode-21054639.

[xxxv]Maggie Lena Walker. (2013). The Biography Channel website. Retrieved 04:13, Dec 16, 2013, from http://www.biography.com/people/maggie-lena-walker-9522099.

[xxxvi]Taylor, Erica, The Tom Joyner Morning Show (2013, March 26), *Little Known Black History Facts: Beatrice "Miss Bea" Borders*, The Black America Web website, (http://blackamericaweb.com/112468/little-known-black-history-fact-beatrice-miss-bea-borders/2/)

[xxxvii]Bessie Coleman. (2013). The Biography Channel website. Retrieved 04:16, Dec 16, 2013, from http://www.biography.com/people/bessie-coleman-36928.

[xxxviii]Ida B. Wells. (2013). The Biography Channel website. Retrieved 04:18, Dec 16, 2013, from http://www.biography.com/people/ida-b-wells-9527635.

[xxxix]Taylor, Erica L., The Tom Joyner Morning Show (2013, August 18), *Little Known Black History Facts: Jackie Ormes*, The Black America Web website, (http://blackamericaweb.com/157728/little-known-black-history-fact-jackie-ormes/2/)

[xl]Gwendolyn Elizabeth Brooks. (2013). The Biography Channel website. Retrieved 04:21, Dec 16, 2013, from http://www.biography.com/people/gwendolyn-brooks-9227599.

[xli]Bellis, Mary, *Bessie Blount - Physical Therapist*, The About.com Inventors website, Retrieved Dec 16, 2013 from http://inventors.about.com/od/bstartinventors/a/Bessie_Blount.htm

[xlii]Johnson, Sandra (2001, August 21) *Annie J. Easley*, The NASA website. Retrieved Dec 16, 2013 from http://www.jsc.nasa.gov/history/oral_histories/NASA_HQ/Herstory/EasleyAJ/EasleyAJ_8-21-01.htm

[xliii]Shirley Chisholm. (2013). The Biography Channel website. Retrieved 04:42, Dec 16, 2013, from http://www.biography.com/people/shirley-chisholm-9247015.

[xliv]Taylor, Erica, The Tom Joyner Morning Show (2013, May 12), *Little Known Black History Facts: Milwaukee's Own Claretta Simpson, Community Activist*, The Black America Web website, (http://blackamericaweb.com/125235/little-known-black-history-fact-milwaukees-own-claretta-simpson-community-activist/2)

[xlv]Wilma Rudolph. (2013). The Biography Channel website. Retrieved 04:43, Dec 16, 2013, from http://www.biography.com/people/wilma-rudolph-9466552.

[xlvi]Taylor, Erica, The Tom Joyner Morning Show (2013, May 23), *Little Known Black History Facts: Elizabeth "Libba" Cotton*, The Black America Web website, (http://blackamericaweb.com/129239/little-known-black-history-fact-elizabeth-libba-cotten/)

Taylor, Erica (2010, February 17), *The evolution of 'cotten picking' Elizabeth 'Libba' Cotton,* The Indianapolis Recorder, (http://www.indianapolisrecorder.com/news/features/article_2a7a638e-7900-54e8-bce0-236482b06f64.html)

[xlvii]Debi Thomas. (2013). The Biography Channel website. Retrieved 04:47, Dec 16, 2013, from http://www.biography.com/people/debi-thomas-537712.

The ABC Sports website. *Wide World of Sports Athletes of the Year.* Retrieved Dec 16, 2013 from http://espn.go.com/abcsports/wwos/athletesoftheyear.html

[xlviii]Mae C. Jemison. (2013). The Biography Channel website. Retrieved 04:57, Dec 16, 2013, from http://www.biography.com/people/mae-c-jemison-9542378.

[xlix] *Composer Biography* Retrieved Dec 16, 2013 from Composer Earnestine Rodgers Robinson website http://www.earnestinerobinson.com/biography.html

[l]Michelle Obama. (2013). The Biography Channel website. Retrieved 05:04, Dec 16, 2013, from http://www.biography.com/people/michelle-obama-307592.

Made in the USA
Columbia, SC
13 February 2022